Liesel Kippen (Lawrence) has had many years of teaching experience in both primary and secondary school settings. She has held leadership positions and has coached, mentored and provided support to teachers in a variety of learning areas (English, writing, mathematics, thinking curriculum and assessment) on a number of educational platforms in her leadership role. Liesel is passionate about writing and has achieved great success in encouraging students to write and enjoy critical thinking experiences. She has demonstrated many exemplary teaching skills to engage students and to support teachers in the teaching of writing. Her Writers' Workshops have been highly successful with Victorian teachers. She has a huge passion for writing and endeavours to share this with her readers.

I'd like to dedicate my book to my family and friends, who have provided encouragement throughout my writing endeavours and who have believed in me every step of the way.

Liesel Kippen

WHISPERS IN TIME

AUSTIN MACAULEY PUBLISHERS™
LONDON • CAMBRIDGE • NEW YORK • SHARJAH

A CIP catalogue record for this title is available from the British Library.

ISBN 9781398427365 (Paperback)
ISBN 9781398427372 (Hardback)
ISBN 9781398427396 (ePub e-book)
ISBN 9781398427389 (Audiobook)

www.austinmacauley.co.uk

First Published 2024
Austin Macauley Publishers Ltd®
1 Canada Square
Canary Wharf
London
E14 5AA

I'd like to say a special thank you to my family who have always been a pillar of strength for me. They are Beatrice Lawrence (mum), Peter Lawrence (dad), Marise Lawrence (sister), Joshua Kippen (son), Adam Kippen (son), Caleb Ogle (nephew) and Joel Ogle (nephew). Thank you so much for everything you have said and done to make my dream a reality. I will forever be indebted to you, my dear family. I am truly grateful and appreciative.

I'd like to add a special note of acknowledgement to Austin Macauley Publishers for their assistance and support throughout the publication process of my book. Thank you for believing in me, for taking a chance with me, for enabling me to accomplish my dream and for enabling me to bring my passion for writing to the fore. Thank you for inspiring me to unleash my creativity and explore my passion for life through my poetry.

Table of Contents

I have a huge passion for writing and enjoy letting my ideas
run wild on a page. My endeavour in life is to encourage,
uplift and motivate. I strive to do this in my writing, and in
all I do and say. I am in awe of nature and its vast treasures.
I receive much pleasure and inspiration from observing
nature in its many beautiful forms. I hope that my writing
can bring out this love and passion I have for nature and its
splendour. I hope to immerse my readers in my thoughts,
descriptions and experiences. I also endeavour to share my
love and passion for life with others through my writing. In
this way, I hope to share a part of me with the world.

1. Life Is Like

Life is like a rose
Waiting to bloom.
Life is like an attic
Filled with gloom.
Life is like a treasure
Costly and rare.
Life is like a friend
Treat it with care.
Life is like a chocolate
Waiting to be had.
Life is like a bad dream
Traumatic and sad.
Life is like an ice cream
Ready to melt.

Life is like a fine cloth
Begging to be felt.
Life is like a sea
Treacherous and vast.
Life is a gamble
Enjoy it to the last.
Life is like a window
Displaying everything in sight.
Life can be a bully
Don't give up without a fight.
As you reflect on this poem
Either today or tonight
Remember that life on the whole
Can be quite all right.

2. COVID Moments

The day has finally dawned,
When my students I will see.
I think of their last day of term,
When they were not filled with glee.
No one could quite comprehend then,
What the future would pan out to be.
Everywhere we turned,
Looked bleak with uncertainty.

Televisions, radios, networks,
And international media too
All spoke of gloom and doom,
And the chaos that would ensue.
Questions were thrown everywhere,
And no answers could be found
For no one at the time,
Had a clue of what was going on around.

Knowledge, then, was limited,
And stories fled quite fast.
Some of us were doubtful,
Of how long this uncertainty would last.
Each had their own version,
Of how matters would unfold.
Some versions were quite interesting
While others daunting, yet bold.

Kiddie-winks finished school on the last day,
While others, some days before.
They all pondered and brainstormed,
About whether schooling would continue any more.
For some, it seemed strangely odd,
A trifle intense and bizarre
That a tiny little virus,
Could travel both near and far.

By then the hysteria had taken root
and the maddening frenzy was in full force
As toilet rolls became the victims,
With everybody hunting for their source.

Madness soon took over,
And selfishness prevailed
As stockpiling took centre stage
And all sanity was derailed.

What started out in China,
Soon moved around really quick.
And in two shakes of a duck's tail,
The entire world began to get sick.
COVID's rounds had begun,
First, in Wuhan's shadows, undetected
But within days it grew bolder
And took the lives of those it affected.

Theories circulated and accelerated,
As countries all shut down.
Lockdown and isolation
Took hold in every town.
Sanitiser and detergents,
Were deemed valuable as gold.
They were hunted down fervently,
In every outlet where they were sold.

People kept their distance,
And were advised to stay at home.
They were not allowed to socialise
Congregate or roam.
Safety measures were put in place,
To lower COVID cases.
These were finally adhered to
As masks were put on faces.

More theories and anecdotes
Addressed COVID-19 hygiene
While everywhere around the globe
COVID's impact could be seen.
The world moved hesitantly and in fear,
As a deep-seated terror took hold.
It seemed like a small number of people
Invited God into their fold.

It soon became apparent
That COVID was here to stay.
That's when fervent prayers were ushered upwards
To God in every way.
Unity, strength and compassion
Became global pivotal tools
As countries sought to communicate,
On how to administer worldwide COVID rules.

One by one each nation,
Began to take a stand
With boldness and confidence
Some with Bibles in their hand.
They braved the many onslaughts
Of politics and more
But little did they know
that another 'avalanche' was in store.

Tired and exhausted,
And weary from it all
Everyone now reminisces,
About how COVID made us fall.

No one would have imagined,
A world abruptly standing still
And sinking solemnly to its knees
While COVID 'killed' and had her fill.

Now Lee could go on and on with this poem
And never completely stop
Because writing is what ignites her fuel,
And keeps her soul on the hop.
However, she'll quench the urge to indulge you,
And stifle her desire to write more
Because today is all students' first day back
With recounts and escapades galore.

3. A Chocolate Explosion of Taste

Her rich and silky-smooth feel
As she slithers gently and easily down the throat,
Is nothing short of nostalgic and euphoric.
Goosebumps subtly begin to emerge
First, as little pores on the skin,
But then, grow more daring and bold.
Before long, these pearly miniature bubbles
Erupt all over the skin's surface.
The silky-smooth edible ball of decadence

Makes its way unhurriedly,
From its point of entry in the mouth
Leaving chocolatey trails on its journey down the throat.

The rich, dark chocolate ball of delight
Continues its downward spiral of sheer pleasure,
Without a fight.
Shivers of joy creep uncaringly and stealthily up the spine.
A tingling sensation lingers for a few pregnant moments,
Maybe nine.
Then suddenly, its deconstruction process takes form,
As the chocolate's delicate exterior begins to melt silently
away:
A norm.
What started out as a solid ball of cocoa palaver
Transforms into a liquid rivulet of chocolate lava.

Her dark brown satiny features
Resemble the rich, tanned colour
And texture of the earth.
One could easily mistake this fluid decadence,
For the earth's muddy contours
After heavy rain.
If not imbued with her addictive
Cappuccino and coffee-flavoured aftertaste,
One would undoubtedly and emphatically proclaim,
As lava oozes from the earth's core
Mantle and crust…
The chocolatey gooeyness of the filling,
Seeps through its core
Like acid poured on rust.

Uncontrolled and untamed,
It unleashes its explosive flavour.
Without warning or hesitation
All decadence breaks loose,
And an indelible taste lingers, to savour.

4. Dawn

The sun stretches forth her hands
Towards the earth.
Her rays seep through the treetops
And display her mirth.

Her glistening arrival
Heralds the dawn of a new day
While caterpillars and snails lie lethargically
Facing each golden ray.

The heavy, bleak darkness
From the night before,
Has made its hurried exit
And for a while, will be seen no more.

A slight breeze makes known her presence
And mumbles its approval of the morning glow
Then gently nudges a few tawny leaves
Lying precariously on the moist, rugged ground below.

Jewelled dewdrops
Gently tip-toe off the leaves
Eager to feel the sun's warmth
And depart from the night's embracing sleeves.

Satiny clouds, sprawled aimlessly
All fluffy, cauliflower-like and grey.
They appear dauntingly and fleetingly
And half threaten to stay.

It looks like heavy showers
Will ruin and spoil the day
But then suddenly and hesitantly
They float grudgingly away.

The sun once again resumes her place
Above the cloudless blue sky above.
The birds begin their chirpy tunes
And a couple whisper words of love.

Dawn has that magical and mystical effect
That warms the heart and soul.
She energises and revitalises
And brings comfort as her goal.

Her beauty and her warmth
Shine through the darkest night
Bringing hope and tranquillity
As her light shines ever so bright.

Her radiance touches the mountains,
The valleys, leaves and trees.
As her golden belt emerges
It forces one to one's knees.

Her fiery orange light
Forms a blanket and a shroud
Creating a vibrant ambience
Powerfully, without being loud.

Dawn's glow decorates the land
And her subtlety decorates the sea.
Her shimmering, glowing glory
Emerges beautifully and unabashedly!

5. Lost Gold Pendant

Reflective,

I am like a mirror.

Fast,

I can make you rich.

Wet,

I can be quite slippery.

Dry,

I can be adorned.

I can be here.

I can be there.

In fact,

I can be anywhere.

But, alas,
If you take the time,
You will find
That I am a unique and rare kind.
I hide not in the mind
But in a school way behind.

Behind the noise.
Behind the classrooms.
Behind the playthings.
I hide behind.

Both trees and plants
Leaves and stones
I lay to rest
In the earth's nest.
Students jump all over me
And yet, I lay, enduringly.

6. Fear

It creeps into your soul
And makes you breathless.
It grips you like a vice
And your actions become reckless.

It robs you of your bliss
It steals your peace of mind.
A scarier emotion
Is a trifle hard to find.

When fear grabs hold of you
It takes away your joy.
It plays havoc with your thoughts
And with your mental state it toys.

It lurks around suspiciously
It feeds cantankerously on your doubts.
It causes you to scream,
To rant around and shout.

Fear silently kills
It subtly destroys.
It's deviously cunning
In all of its treacherous ploys.

Fear can be deceitful
It certainly knows its craft.
Its perfidious nature
Pierces like a shaft.

When fear descends upon you
Don't invite it to stay.
Promptly guide it to the door
And send it miles away.

7. Love

Love is like a wall
Solid and sure.
Love is like medicine
Ready to cure.

Love is like a fire
Warm at first, then hot.
When love moves boldly in
It finds the heart's most vulnerable spot.

Love is a soothing balm
A remedy for sad emotions.
When the right ingredients are added
You have a powerfully potent potion.

Love knows how to build up
It always seeks to inspire.
When these two are entwined
It creates ripples of passion and desire.

Love is always caring
It eagerly aims to please.
It seldom tries to hurt or harm
Or tease and cause unease.

Love is a noteworthy survivor
Even with its many flaws.
When faced with challenges and obstacles
It stands resiliently through those wars.

Love's beauty is rare
Its steadfastness, a treasure.
Combined with its compassionate nature,
Having true love, is a pleasure.

Critics and cynics have their thoughts
On how love can be blind.
This has an element of truth
And can somewhat confuse the mind.

If love is not patient
Respectful or kind,
Then the type of love secured
Is not that 'sought-after' and rare find.

Love should be sentimental
It should fill you with glowing awe.
Constant gushes of raw and steamy emotions
Should explode from within the heart's core.

Love should seek to ravish
In a tender and loving embrace,
While all other lesser emotions
Disappear without a trace.

Love should be passionate
Sometimes untamed and raw
Guided by solid and authentic feelings
That are untarnished and pure.

The pure, eternal and everlasting love
Can never be bought or sold.
It endures through life's torturous ages.
Its endurance, in many tales, is told.

Love can be quite complex
It's often confused with lust.
If the heart does not decipher soon
Those feelings will corrode like rust.

Love is a deep commitment
An intense affection, it ignites.
When faced with trials and tribulations
Love overcomes all odds and fights.

Love is a priceless treasure
It's beautifully and intricately bold.
When nursed and cared for sacredly
Love is worth its weight in gold.

8. Mask

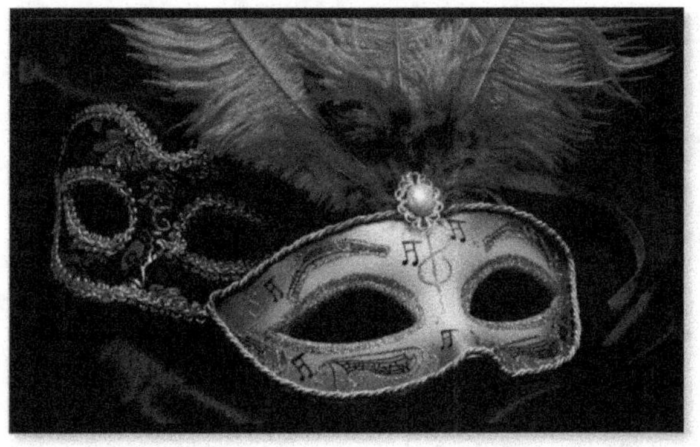

These masks that we wear
Form a cloak around our soul.
They camouflage emotions
Burnt black like coal.
They hide all the sorrow
From life's many wars.
Bitterness and anguish
Form festered, contagious sores.

These masks that we wear
Veil emotions hidden deep.
Those that lie dormant
For which we quietly weep.

They disguise our very essence
Of things we hold quite dear.
Because the slightest disclosure
Attracts unwarranted fear.

These masks that we wear
Are visors for our mind.
They shut out adversity
And stresses of every kind.
They numb the brain covertly
Hiding behind a visage of joy,
While dressing up the façade
In a disposition coquettishly coy.

These masks that we wear
Our immune system's lair
Shelters a scantily shaded,
Unguarded and steely stare.
Their flimsy fragile makeup
A thinly layered shield.
Strategically protective mechanisms
Of infinite power, they wield.

These masks that we wear
Conceal our innermost thoughts
Plagued by infinite sadness
And marred by irreparable onslaughts.
They hover, captured in a realm
Of cognitive control,
Where, in solitude, they mourn
Disguised in a faceless role.

These masks that we wear
Take on many different forms
Those that weather atrocities
And life's horrific storms.
They barricade anxiety
And blockade extreme pain,
While quietly soothing
And rehabilitating the self again.

These masks that we wear
Are lifesaving tools.
Without these vital implements
We'd drown in life's cesspools.
They embellish our expressions
Add fillers to our frowns,
While our smiles broadly dazzle
With gold decorated crowns.

9. Nature's Grandeur

A beautiful setting dominates the scene
Magnificent shades on nature's wide screen.
A mystic presence hovers around
A more majestic ambience can ne'er be found.

An enchanting woodland, peculiarly grand
Sublimely exquisite, in some far-off land,
Where civilisation has not yet touched
Nor human eye fixedly watched.

This tranquil forest breathes life to all
For creatures and birds both great and small.
They find their solace in these colourful arrays
Of turquoise, lilac and subtle greys.

Reddish tones and light brown too
Olive greens and aqua blue,
Dominant pink, all enhance the view
While oyster creams sprawl lethargically on cue.

Aubergine trees, antique teal
With a semi-rugged, leathery feel,
Point upwards, bending towards the sun
As radiant heat descends on each one.

Complex patterns of a whistled note
Are sung in tune as if by rote.
Melodious ensembles, beautifully rare
From a solitary lark without a care.

Sagging branches from weeping willows
Form drooping clusters of leafy pillows.
Delicate pink cherry blossoms
Camouflage miniscule squirrel-like possums.

The clouds above conceal the sky
Voluminous, puffy and nestled on high.
Hazy, bluish and well-defined
These candy floss wisps are one of a kind.

Mirrored waters, jewelled below
Quietly echo life's ebb and flow.
Their limpid features duplicate
Nature's splendorous, beauteous, timeless state.

10. We Rise

We rise, though our foes seek fame.
We rise, while victories, they hope to gain.
We rise, though utterances they proclaim.
We rise!

We rise, in spite of the pain.
We rise, amidst all the shame.
We rise, though our lives aren't the same.
We rise!

We rise, though our spirits they tame.
We rise, though our identity they claim.
We rise, though our nature they frame.
We rise!

We rise, though we're considered insane.
We rise, though we've abandoned our aim.
We rise, though our dreams have been slain.
We rise!

We rise, when we've forgotten our name.
We rise, with our captive ball and chain.
We rise, with a confused brain.
We rise!

We rise, though our bodies are lame.
We rise, while blood pumps through our vein.
We rise, on a cognitive plane.
We rise!

We rise, through every purgerous lane.
We rise, above nepotism's reign.
We rise, through authoritarian strain.
We rise!

We rise, above the corporate gravy train.
We rise, like medicinal vervain.
We rise, life's cellular membrane.
We rise!

We rise, like an English quatrain.
We rise, like a whipped candy cane.
We rise, while life seeks to drain.
We rise!

We rise, with our motley matted mane.
We rise, while choked on our rein.
We rise, on every unbalanced domain.
We rise!

We rise, like adrenalin caffeine.
We rise, bruised by life's chicane.
We rise, with minimal complain.
We rise!

We rise, drenched in suffering's stain.
We rise, pitted against the inhumane.
We rise, above the corporate political campaign.
We rise!

We rise, far from the mundane.
We rise, precariously unslain.
We rise, on semi-wobbly terrain.
We rise!

We rise, above society's Egyptian henbane.
We rise, tangled like chicken Chow Mein.
We rise, tenacious like Fort Wayne.
We rise!

We rise, like oxygenated lutein.
We rise, through hardship's torrential rain.
We rise, like oozing champagne.
We rise!

We rise, like powerfully charged methane.
We rise, from the bottom of life's food chain.
We rise, with no semblance of disdain.
We rise!

11. Despair

Tossed about
Swollen.
Knocked out
Fallen.
Sadness takes hold.
Battered.
Tattered.
Shattered.
The body is bruised and cold.

Despondency discreetly takes root
Spreading its tentacles like a bamboo shoot.
Dismal thoughts overwhelm
Melancholy, steadfast at the helm.

Pressed down
Suffocated.
Forced to the ground
Annihilated.
Life's heavy load takes its toll.
Breathless.
Motionless.
Lifeless.
Drained from it all.

Hopes and dreams burn to the ground
Feelings of helplessness all around.
Desolation ravages the soul.
Nothing tangible will make it whole.

12. The Lake District

A satiny mist descends over the Lake
Her profound beauty, breathtaking…no fake.
Silvery, cotton wool hangs over the land
Made infinitely by God's loving hand.

The shroud sits majestically on high
Reigning supremely in an opaque sky.
Faint, feathery, sleepy and white
Morning has broken after the dreary night.

Clouds nestle in nature's arms below
In the forested, myriads of trees that grow.
This beautifully fragrant forest air
Emits a scent so delicately rare.

Sweet and smoky, inebriating smells
A strong and earthy pungent dwell.
Delicately seductive and distinctly faint
These authentic odours acutely taint.

Enormous trees, fern-like and green
Autumn colours, even tangerine.
Grand and leafy titanic heights
All bask in the sun's raw golden lights.

Ancient, rugged, shaggy and tall
Orange trees, crimson and small.
Sustained images of beauty unfold
As the subtle nuances of daybreak takes hold.

Flowering plants, alluringly adorned
With protective involucre, fleetingly scorned.
The height from the trees enlarges the view
While shadows and colours permeate on cue.

Well-kept lawns and neatly trimmed grass
Encapsulates a mass of filmy glass.
Its gauze-like features and liquid state
Creates a lake so elegantly ornate.

Chirping birds provide a musical interlude
Tweets so profound, they graciously soothe.
Unconstrained and unrehearsed
While Windermere's poets add these to their verse.

The rolling hills of the countryside
Are lavishly sprawled on landscapes, wide.
They subtly keep quiet profiles
As nature's grandeur stockpiles.

Imposing landforms, this scenic place
Displays her trinkets with modest grace.
England's District Lake, a literary treasure
Hides untold wealth of infinite measure.

13. Life's Musical Tunes

Jangling of chains
From a dog on a leash,
It growls and grunts
When you tug at his quiche.

Swerving and curving
As the car takes a bend,
The screeching of brakes
Heralds the journey's abrupt end.

Shuffling of feet
On a cobbled stony road,
The frail tottering man
Succumbs to his load.

Sizzling of oil
In a well-greased pan,
Spicy peppered sausages
Tossed and turned by nan.

Popping and clicking
From a solitary fish,
Whose caudal fin flexes
In a pellucid dish.

Crinkling of paper
And squashed in a ball,
The author's written attempts
Now, a futile scrawl.

The howling of the wind
On a cold winter's night,
Prompts the huddling together
Under covers and out of sight.

A tapping at the windows
From the pitter patter of rain,
Causes droplets to gently trickle
And dance alluringly on the crystal pane.

14. Sweetest Song of Love

The sweetest of all sounds come from a tree
As a nightingale sings beautifully.
He sings to his love, his destined fate
Who has won his heart, his true love and soul mate?

My alluring love, my beauty be
Oh, won't you hear my melody.
I sing to you, my heart's true key
You, who unlocks happiness for me.

No other maiden has captured my heart
You stole it right from the very start.
You evoke my joy, you touch my soul
With you I feel piously whole.

I sing to you, in whistled tunes
Those amorous notes above the dunes.
I sing at night, when all is still
My heart beats steadily for you, at will.

Oh, to you, my warm-blooded, light-winged queen
You, on whose love I securely lean.
I serenade my Eros amore
To the one whose beauty I adore.

These nocturnal notes, for you, this ode
No other love shall know our code.
Dedicated to my chosen one
For whom, there's no comparison, under the sun.

Your alluring beauty, a dazzling thing
It prompts me to want to dance and sing.
Up in the boughs beyond the green
Where all of nature can be seen.

Oh, fly with me above the trees
You, who brings me to my knees.
From May to June, I'm in full song
From dawn to dusk, for you I long.

15. When Love Gently Knocks

Your wistful smile
That causes your eyes to crinkle
And muscles to flex in the apples of your cheeks
Lazy and relaxed.

Your jubilant laughter
Bubbling infectiously on us all
Beautifully adorable and one of a kind
Which prompts me to laugh warmly and heartily
And simply blows my mind.

It brews deep down
At the heart's core
The quintessence of feelings, raw
Then makes its way from the floor
To the surface…the body's door.

That flirty giggle
Transforming into a booming laugh
Your frame gently vibrates
And your shoulders start to shake
The kind of love that makes my heart quietly ache.

Tears of joy flood your eyes
An endearing and heart-warming disguise
Your arms wrap themselves around your face
As you playfully tumble onto the floor's space.

I get vacuumed in your warm embrace
Here, I find my special resting place
When love gently knocks on the heart's door
It touches the soul's most intimate and sentimental core.

16. The Break of Dawn

The night's quiet has slowly waned
Morning has waltzed casually in.
She brings with her lethargy, feigned
And dawn's golden glow, her kin.
As darkness's curtain rises up
It instantly dissipates
Into the sky's fleecy clouds
Where heaven's carpet awaits.

In its place beautifully descends
A subtle morning glow.
It hovers gently over all
And puts on a splendid show.
The oyster white trail it leaves behind

Dances in flimsy transparent leaps
Then spreads its negligee arms
Subtly, and through the trees it seeps.

A radiant golden glow peeks in
Above the rugged hills.
It comfortably rests betwixt the mounds
Then on those mountains, it kneels.
Its glory shines in blinding spurts
A blazing sphere takes form.
All of nature bow their heads
And to its beauty, they warm.

17. A Starry Night (Shape Poem)

Luminous balls of gas

Beautify the night.

Their penetrating glare

Spread magnificent shards of white.

Splintered fragmented rays

Dominate the darkened skies.

These globules of effervescent shapes

Emit patterns that galvanise.

Evening's impenetrable cloak

Shatters from their piercing poke.

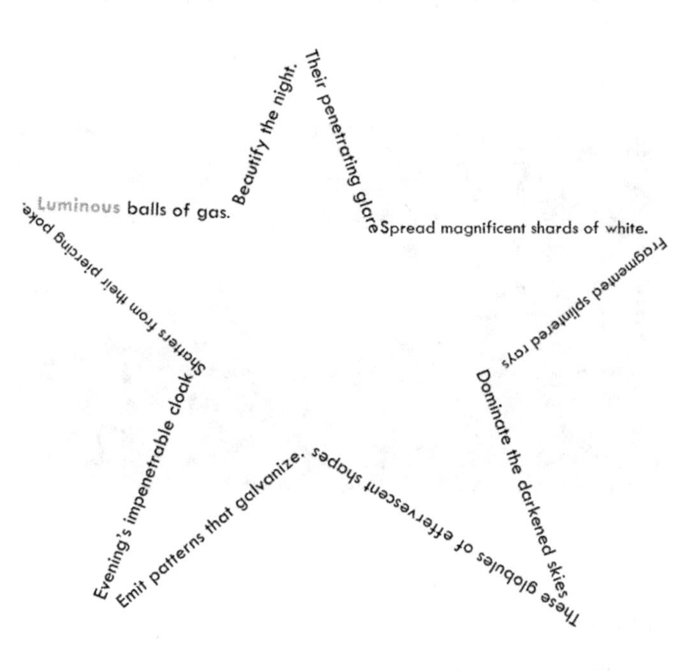

Their penetrating glare
Spread magnificent shards of white.
Beautify the night.
Luminous balls of gas.
Shatters from their piercing poke.
Evening's impenetrable cloak
Emit patterns that galvanize.
These globules of effervescent shapes
Dominate the darkened skies
Fragmented splintered rays

18. Splashes of Colour

A walk through the forest on a warm summer's day
One can't help but gasp at nature's awesome display.
Colours majestically float all around
Their impact acknowledged, without uttering a sound.
Careful mixtures of crimson and grey
With a dollop of gold from the sun's piercing ray.
A sprinkling of brown fills part of the view
Each day, magnificence and splendour anew.
Reds spill over and gently infiltrate
Without attempting to dominate.
They blend in subtly with the shades of green
From olive to lime and vibrant evergreen.
A beautiful lushness serenades the ground

Oozing voluptuousness and luxuriance all around.
Copious amounts of towering trees
Fill the many vacant spots with ease.
A silvery lustrous greyish-white light
Shimmers and sparkles specks remarkably bright.

19. Rise Above

Life has many obstacles
That challenge us each day.
They seek to ultimately destroy us
In every possible way.
We often try to fathom
The nature of their aim
Or why they are determined
To decimate us in life's game.

We can never fully comprehend
Why these obstacles are around.
All they seem devised for

Is to cripple without a sound.
Everything we hold dear
They subtly intimidate
And deceivingly manipulate
By consuming us with their hate.

We never fully grasp it all
Why this has become our fate
That experiences we live through
Strive to dominate.
They course through our bodies
And infiltrate our minds
Surging with a vengeance
And negativity of every kind.

Life knows how to knock us down
A skill it most enjoys
Often finding pleasure
While, with our thoughts, it toys.
It never seems satisfied
Until we are completely undone
Then it defiantly accumulates
Victories from us that it has won.

Now we can sit and ponder
Why life stubbornly takes its toll
Or pacify our thinking
While deliberating on a knoll.
We could quietly sit by

And let life have the edge
Or we could rise boldly
And strategically erect a hedge.

We could put a stop to events of life
That are soaked with evil intent
And sometimes, if need be
Find a quiet spot to vent.
Then rise above the obstacles
And tower over their might
While determining within ourselves
Not to give in without a fight.

As we take charge of our life
And brave its many wars
We'll finally reach our destination
On quieter, calmer shores.
We'll develop a disposition
Of powerful character and strength
As we rise above everything
In height, depth, width and length.

20. Looking Through the Eyes of Love

Looking through the eyes of love
What do you see?
Sparking eyes of tenderness
That enlarge so beautifully.

Looking through the eyes of love
What do you see?
An erased frown, no longer creased
And now completely free.

Looking through the eyes of love
What do you see?
An elegant, well-designed nose
That breathes life appreciatively.

Looking through the eyes of love
What do you see?
Rosy cheeks with crimson tints
Smiling radiantly.

Looking through the eyes of love
What do you see?
Dainty little puffed out lips
Singing tunes jubilantly.

Looking through the eyes of love
What do you see?
A genuine smile that radiates
For all the world to see.

Looking through the eyes of love
What do you see?
Ears delicate and receptive
Listening sympathetically.

Looking through the eyes of love
What do you see?
Kindness in expression
That shines outwardly.

Looking through the eyes of love
What do you see?
Arms clasped in a loving embrace
Hugging amorously.

Looking through the eyes of love
What do you see?
A caring and compassionate, tender heart
Sharing love unconditionally.

Looking through the eyes of love
What do you see?
Legs striding towards a goal
Gliding decisively.

21. Crimson Sunset

The day has closed its curtains
Evening has comfortably settled in.
She saunters about lethargically
Attired in radiantly warm skin.
Her romantically tranquil presence
Oozes opulence and grace
As she sets about transforming
The sky's darkened sunset face.

Shades of purple gather around
Sprinkled with a brilliant red haze.
Lilac shades take centre stage
And set the skies ablaze.
A fiery trail hovers above
Forming rivulet patterns of pink.
Auburn streaks tiptoe in
As the setting sun quietly sinks.

Flaming gorgeous colours
Unfold lavishly onto the scene
As tempestuous, suave scarlets
Dominantly lean.
Wickedly glorious lavender
Gently secures its place
Nestled between the luminous contours
Of the sky's dark and brazen face.

The tumultuously dynamic setting
Beautifies the shore
While a solitary tree observes
This majestic glow in awe.
It quietly feeds upon the rays
And basks in their ambience
Then sheds its own beautiful glow
An apocalyptic and stormy red nuance.

22. Feline Stalker

Glassy eyes
Steely stare.
Frozen look
Penetrating glare.
Narrow focus
Daggered pupils.
Silver-grey feline
No scruples.

Deliberating.
Cogitating.
Meditating.
Contemplating.

Flank crouched
Back arched.
Head stretched
Mouth parched.
Ears twitched
Nostrils flared.
Predator pounced
Prey ensnared.

23. Out of the Ashes We Rise

Against all odds, we persevere
Amidst all pain, we thrive.
Through the challenges, we shed a tear
But out of the ashes we rise.

Life knows how to knock us down
And drag us to the hilt.
It attacks our very inner core
And leaves us there to wilt.
Our bodies lack the energy.
Our voices lack the sounds.
Our hearts lack all feeling.
Obstacles are devilishly on their rounds.

Against all odds, we persevere
Amidst all pain, we thrive.
Through the challenges, we shed a tear
But out of the ashes we rise.

Life robs us of our euphoric joy.
It takes away our peace.
Then seeks to imprison us
In cells that have no keys.
It strives to dismantle
And unhinge our settled state
With intimidation that unnerves,
Propagates and incites hate.

Against all odds, we persevere
Amidst all pain, we thrive.
Through the challenges, we shed a tear
But out of the ashes we rise.

Life's obstacles are brutally bold
They storm their way right in.
Every area of our life
They are deviously determined to win.
They brutishly devour
Any vestige of sanity
And fervently gnaw at
All forms of modest vanity.

Against all odds, we persevere
Amidst all pain, we thrive.
Through the challenges, we shed a tear
But out of the ashes we rise.

Adversity comes in all forms
It doesn't discriminate.
Its goal is to handicap
Destroy or devastate.
Unending torment and oppression
Agonising misery and pain,
Torturous suffering and deprivation
Wrapped up in sadness and shame.

Against all odds, we persevere
Amidst all pain, we thrive.
Through the challenges, we shed a tear
But out of the ashes we rise.

Challenges seek to consume us
Demolish and annihilate
Attacking our thought processes
As we collapse under their weight.
They ridicule, they chide.
They ostracise, quite snide.
They dominate, they grip.
They injure, they rip.

Against all odds, we persevere
Amidst all pain, we thrive.
Through the challenges, we shed a tear
But out of the ashes we rise.

While dazed upon the ground we lie
Breathless from it all.
We analyse our mishaps
And how obstacles caused our fall.
While aggressively seeking to ravage
And painstakingly ensnare.
All that they served to achieve
Was a temporary rip and tear.

Against all odds, we persevere
Amidst all pain, we thrive.
Through the challenges, we shed a tear
But out of the ashes we rise.

Momentarily knocked off our feet
Or pinned against a wall,
These challenges of life
Have enabled us to stand tall.
They've sharpened our character
Our resilience, now the prison of Fort Knox.
Their delusional plans to control us
Inside life's deplorable box.

Against all odds, we persevere
Amidst all pain, we thrive.
Through the challenges, we shed a tear
But out of the ashes we rise.

They've pushed us to our limits
Until we've reached our max.
Our breaking point now visited
And evident from our tracks.
Through it all we've endured
And survived every foiled attack.
We've sustained the many onslaughts
With scars sketched raw on our back.

Against all odds, we persevere
Amidst all pain, we thrive.
Through the challenges, we shed a tear
But out of the ashes we rise.

From life's many experiences
We've learnt a thing or two,
Those harbouring ill-feelings
Disempowers and impairs us too.
Challenges have made us strong
They've developed our inner strength.
Life has become more meaningful
In breadth, width and length.

Against all odds, we persevere
Amidst all pain, we thrive.
Through the challenges, we shed a tear
But out of the ashes we rise.

While we can't change our experiences
We can learn from them and grow.
They have shaped our varied perspectives
And have enhanced all that we know.
Out of circumstance's fiery flames
We've been forged from tenacious stuff,
Made to withstand pressure
Like a chiselled diamond in the rough.

Against all odds, we persevere
Amidst all pain, we thrive.
Through the challenges, we shed a tear
But out of the ashes we rise.

Life's challenges may have crippled us
But our temperance remains,
Where we can laugh in adversity's face
And smile at all our new-found gains.
Having ventured through the fires
We've been reborn like pure gold,
Celebrating our enthralling victories
From the burnt ashes, these phoenixes emerge bold.

Against all odds, we persevere
Amidst all pain, we thrive.
Through the challenges, we shed a tear
But out of the ashes we rise.

Against all odds, we persevere
Amidst all pain, we thrive.
Through the challenges, we shed a tear

BUT OUT OF THE ASHES WE RISE!

24. King of the Skies

It soars above on wings of steel
This powerful bird of the skies.
It cuts through the air seamlessly
And glides as it skilfully flies.
No flapping of wings, this eagle needs
To soar with grace and flair.
By changing the position of its wings
This machine dominates the air.

An eagle's wings are a sight to behold
They are powerfully made for flight.
As it flies with turbo-powered speed
The feathers display their might.
They spread themselves towards the wind

Slicing the air with their edges.
Then masterfully using their wide surfaces
They slow down their movement, like wedges.

They soar and glide above the clouds
A majestic view from below.
As they powerfully rise into the air
Eagles put on a spectacular show.
With heads outstretched and eyes alert
They focus on their plight
Then circle the skies around them
When their prey comes into sight.

Their wings lie horizontally
Their bodies a perpendicular fit
Their padded thighs tucked under
Like a snugly comfortable quilt.
With the aqua skies behind them
And fleecy clouds around,
These phenomenal, solitary creatures
Soar robustly without a sound.

Eagles have astounding tenacity
They rise above the storm
While other birds seek shelter
And a place to keep themselves warm.
An eagle displays perspicacity;
Clear vision and insight.
It has courage, strength and power
Once a symbol of Roman might.

25. Gone but Not Forgotten

The maiden stood on the wooden platform
Saying her final goodbyes on the dock.
The mood had turned a quiet sombre
The setting near an iconic rock.
Ripples of water surrounded her
Bubbling melodious, tranquil tunes,
While silently raging within her
Was her life now completely in ruins.

She had recently lost the love of her life
A short distance from where she now stood.
His lifeless body had floated above
Close to the dock's peeled wood.

She had tried all she could when it happened
To revive his lifeless state,
But all her efforts to save him
Couldn't stop his traumatic fate.

His passing that day was a painful one
One that she'll always remember.
It was one of those fatal afternoons
A spring day in September.
He had always vowed to learn to swim,
But had never quite found the time
Throughout his active teenage years
And now, well into his prime.

As the maiden reminisces absorbingly
On their countless moments shared
She thinks back on the blissful times
Where he had shown he really cared.
He had showered her with love each day
Had made her feel quite whole.
Love's embers had burned fiercely,
Scorching deeply into her soul.

Now as she ponders on it all
Under the romantic sky,
She is thankful for the life they had
But can't help asking, "Why?"
Why did it have to end this way?
Why had life been so cruel?
Surely, such a terrible fate
Was against any of life's rules?

For now, she'll have to contemplate
On how to rise again,
From her tragically saddened state
To one above the pain.
She'll cherish every amorous thought
That her time with him had brought.
While he may no longer be around
Gone, but not forgotten, plagued her dominant thought.

26. Love Is Like a Butterfly

Love is like a butterfly
Soothingly gentle and calm.
It hovers over flowers
With no intention to harm.

Love is like a butterfly
With striking colour displays.
Its infinitely intricate facets
In many of life's roles, play.

Love is like a butterfly
Whose wings shimmer in the sun.
Love's many attractive features
Can enticingly dazzle one.

Love is like a butterfly
That quietly lingers around.
When it ultimately finds its soul mate
It resides there without a sound.

Love is like a butterfly
Whose beautiful colour camouflages.
Even when consumed with sadness
Through love's door, joy courageously barges.

Love is like a butterfly
Whose compassionate nature shines.
It always seeks to protect
And caringly follows empathy's signs.

Love is like a butterfly
Always on the move,
Scouting for innovative ways
To dress up and enhance its groove.

Love is like a butterfly
Quietly observant,
Casting an affectionate eye
With tenderness, fervent.

Love is like a butterfly
Fleetingly transient.
Love's ephemeral stages
Are transitionally valiant.

Love is like a butterfly
Delicate and warm.
Though love has many types
Eros prompts passionate transform.

Love is like a butterfly
Whimsical and free.
It floats about everywhere
Beautifully nonchalantly.

27. Home's Sanctuary

Home's sanctuary…
Where the soul finds solace
And the mind receives rest.
Where the fatigued bones relax
From a physically draining test.
Where the limbs succumb
On an upholstered headrest,
Beneath a comfy pillow
In brocaded silk, dressed.
Where the muscles contract
That have been compressed
By an elastic bandage

Wrapped firmly around the chest.
Where the body performs
At its flawless best,
And unharnessed feelings
Are no longer suppressed.
Where the worries of the moment
Are adequately addressed,
And the day's successes
Are reassuringly reassessed.
Where the matters of the heart
Are brazenly expressed,
And where life on the whole
Is beautifully blessed.

28. Nature's Sanctum Sanctorum

Harmonious placidity on the land.

Not a scuffle.

Not a brawl.

Not a scamper.

Not a crawl.

Nature's composed repose.

Quiet calm on the tree.

Not a rustle.

Not a shake.

Not a sway.

Not a break.

Nature's reverie and sanctuary.

Deathly silence on the waters.
Not a bubble.
Not a splash.
Not a ripple.
Not a crash.
Nature's petite retreat.

Gentle quietude in the air.
Not a flutter.
Not a shriek.
Not a flapping.
Not a squeak.
Nature's heavenly realm.

29. When Lightning Strikes

A fascinating sight to behold
Is when lightning takes to the skies
And strikes bold.
Out of a cloudless blue hood
Begins to emerge and brood
A darkish grey sombre mood.
Tingling sensations are felt on the hand
As hair begins to rise and stand.
The ear detects a subtle sound
Quiet buzzing and hissing
In its inner mound.

A sudden flash rips through the skies
Tearing to shreds the quietness that lies.
A silvery hot rod follows in tow
Emitting a powerful electrically charged flow.
An explosion of light with its blinding glare
Threatens to incinerate eyes that stare.
The booming echo of a thunderous roar
Sends palpitations that pulsate the heart's core.

Lightning streaks permeate with flair
Forming patterns of irregular branches in the air.
Bony, scraggy, scrawny lines, rare
Resembling wisps of matted and unkempt hair.
Its jagged features waltz on a cloud
While its forks dominate and loom casually, proud.
Incandescent with rage, it lets out a burst
On a shrivelled-up tree, attacked the worst.

From the cumulonimbus puff, it bolts
Unleashing its fury as it vaults,
Somersaulting in a downward spiral
Lightning's energy dispensed and now gone viral.
What remains in view glowing crimson bright
Are golden embers set alight.
The blackened shards from the tree's scarred remains
Protrude defiantly as a lightning stain.
As the embers flicker and lap at the bark
The lightning dissipates, leaving an indelible mark.

30. The Sweetest of Sounds

The sweetest of all sounds comes from a tree
From birds singing melodiously.
Sometimes low, sometimes high
Their notes meander through the sky.
The tweets we've come to know so well
Beautifully calm and stresses quell.
They fill us with a sense of peace
Which therapeutically puts us at ease.
On early mornings we lethargically rise
As the nightingale's tunes bring tears to our eyes.
Combined with whistles, gurgles and trills
We receive a symphony of endearing thrills.
The most beautiful song comes from the thrush

Who woos its listeners; making them radiantly blush.
Some birds have a metallic sound
To communicate messages all around.
Cardinals chime a lilting pitch
Creating an ambience, authentically rich.
These rhythmic sounds of chirps and cheeps
Ignite a world where music speaks.

31. Homeward Bound

I walk towards my home where I feel free
Where I can lie lethargically.
Where all my troubles are swept away
And all my heartaches through a golden ray
Are quietly dispelled and no longer torment
Their hold on my heart now gently rent.
Staring ahead, my vision is clear
Fixated on that familiar dwelling, near.

Closer and closer I meander through
All the snowflakes, ice and dew.
Thick layers sprawled about
Hiding the ground and keeping warmth out.
My old, rugged and quaint home

A source of comfort, I no longer roam.
Burning brightly is her light
Guiding me through this 'blizzardous' night.

Slowly and effortlessly, I make my way
Determined to no longer stray
From her protective realm and fortress walls
And her empty, but cosy, welcoming halls.
Shabby and derelict, a ramshackle abode
But inside holds a heartwarming load.
A bundle of joy and a pillar of strength
My rock, my refuge, my peace at length.

www.ingramcontent.com/pod-product-compliance
Lightning Source LLC
Chambersburg PA
CBHW071458030726
47593CB00003B/1053